A Guide to Golf

How to get out of your own way

By Sam Hale

Contents

For my family and Emily

Prologue

Golf didn't cross my radar until the age of thirteen; before that, most of my attention was directed at playing rugby and tennis and practising judo. I had a well-established history of starting a new venture with great enthusiasm, only to swiftly lose interest, until the day my grandparents introduced me to golf. Being a notoriously expensive sport, my parents hesitated to dive in with a significant initial investment; they made my next task proving my commitment.

In the interim, my grandparents proved to be my biggest supporters. After murdering many hundred balls on the driving range, I felt prepared to put my golfing prowess on full display to my parents. This was the first of many times golf has failed to love me back. It picked me up and dumped me flat on my back when the exhibition surpassed humbling and went straight to horrible.

Nonetheless, the embarrassment left me undeterred, and it wasn't long before a few great shots took me straight back into the pursuit of unattainable perfection. One school holiday, I started hounding my parents to take me to the golf course every day, and they obliged, likely sensing that my obsession had picked up some momentum. Golf had proven to have a unique ability to capture so much of my attention; there was simply no attention left to worry about trivial things, so golf became my greatest refuge. At school, I was not a model student; I was smart enough to get by but didn't do well with rules or structure. When I got in trouble, my parents did as expected and suspended my privileges as a deserved punishment. Interestingly, golf was explicitly off the table regarding disciplinary matters. Perhaps they couldn't stomach such cruel and unusual punishment, or it simply didnt seem wise to take away the one thing I could focus on.

Three years on, I was at a zero handicap. At that point, I declared my intention to be a professional one day. I was immediately presented with several different pathways to achieving my goal. One option was to recognise that I was already pretty good, and since my swing looked okay, I should keep doing exactly what I was doing. Why mess with success? This then brought to the surface another issue: to take such a passive approach was, and still is, against my nature. I felt so far from my goal of being a professional golfer, that it was difficult to see a pathway to reaching it. This experience left me wide open to a more aggressive option. Re-build my swing from start to finish, in that order, one position at a time. I was informed that my body couldn't perform the swing positions essential to professional success. Regular physio, statistics and an extensive practice routine would now become my life. After a few painful physio sessions and stretching, which never seemed to lower my score, I was left disenchanted and further detached from my vision. The prerequisites to such a professional pathway at the time were six months of physio and swing building. This seemed like a lifetime to seventeen-year-old me, so my interest slowly dissipated over time. No matter how many people told me my swing looked great and that I should stop tinkering with it, I didn't manage that until much later.

I soon quit golf to dive head first into becoming an adult. I moved to Australia at the age of 18 to work in oil and gas. After three years of working from before dawn till after dusk in the Central Queensland heat, I left armed with a few creative swear words and a questionable attempt at a beard. I had managed to save enough money to travel the world for a couple of years, so that's exactly what I did. Golf soon became a distant memory and served only as bar talk. Unbeknownst to me, I was developing a skill that would do much more for me than a good golf swing. The ability to communicate and relate to others is the foundation of coaching. However, the only coaching I did at the time involved throwing ping pong balls at red cups.

After an adventurous few years, I returned to New Zealand. At the time, I had zero intention of returning to golf. A favourite pastime of my grandad was watching me at the driving range, so for old times' sake, we went to the local range where we bumped into an old coach of mine. My grandad asked him if any jobs were available, which I thought was a joke (if it was, the coach wasn't in on it). Later that day, I got a call from a manager offering me a job at a driving range. I had little interest, but my savings were getting dangerously low, so I accepted. I suppose my Grandad knew something I didn't because golf roped me back in not long after.

This job led to me applying for the Professional Golfers Association (PGA) Traineeship Program. The PGA program is challenging in many ways, and for me, the most challenging aspect was that to graduate each year, I had to meet the requirement to average under 4.75 over par after 20 rounds. On top of working full-time selling golf clubs and coaching part-time, my life became demanding again. I was coaching more than what was practical, trying to improve my own game, and was forced to learn how to work smarter. I was accustomed to long hours but not to the unique sensation of being passionate about what I was doing. I learned to be patient, not out of virtue but of necessity. I had not yet managed to squeeze the results out of the many swing theories I had studied. When I began coaching, my focus shifted to getting results for my clients. This gave me some much-needed perspective and put me in a position to step back and work out what was in my way.

Chapter 1
Chasing Lasers

The other day, I bought a laser light toy for our cat. He wasted no time in eagerly pursuing the dancing red dot, only for it to slip away again and again. Observing this initially, I was intrigued by his eagerness despite such futility. It didn`t make much sense to continue a pursuit that had never been successful. Albert Einstein defines this as insanity. Apparently, Einstein never played golf. In some cases, like that of the cat, it`s just pure instinct to do something repeatedly.

It occurred to me that I had often been stuck in my own self-made loop in pursuit of simple solutions. The closest I ever got was when a subtle change showed a flicker of promise. No matter how hard I tried, I never managed to capture that laser. It's a valuable instinct to want to be better and chase targets but how do you figure out what target is worth the chase? There is no shortage of information for golfers looking to improve their game or an aspect of it. A Google search will provide countless resources on the correct grip, stance, and posture. The internet offers the perfect medium for famous golf coaches to distribute innovative swing theories to the masses. However, even if you were to come across the best information for you from the most brilliant golf coach in the world, meaningful improvement is far from guaranteed. A market saturated with technical theories and big promises suck up all the air in the golf improvement space. Golfers have become conditioned to operate almost exclusively in technical theory and neglect to consider how best to actually change their technique.

The golf swing and its many forms are an intriguing part of the game; it`s a golfer`s quest for the Holy Grail. The pursuit of which can leave essential aspects such as course management and mental preparedness underdeveloped. Ironically it also makes it much harder to improve your golf swing.

At the beginning of a golf lesson, I like to discuss with the client what they hope to achieve during our time together. Most express their desire for lower scores in some way or another so this logically leads to assessing and then improving their course management, short game, mental skills and possibly some light swing work. I have proudly delivered this to clients many times, yet a little too often they seemed ill-content with themselves at the finish line. I wondered if many clients might be more fulfilled chasing a different target. It's challenging to interpret your average golfer's true goal; even still, I'm starting to think that most golfers' true dream is to strike a golf ball at a level consistent with their perceived ability. In other words, a feeling that they are on the way to using their body's potential. Anything short of this will have them searching for answers from those who make the boldest claims.

Assuming the correct target, logic would then suggest a good place to start might be to emulate the best golfer in their community or a professional on TV. The effectiveness of this strategy depends mainly on what you choose to observe. A golf swing and its various "positions" can be better understood as visual representations of movement skills. The concept of learning golf in a more fluid and fun way has undoubtedly become a focal point of the modern PGA program. Games are used for children to promote the learning of fundamental movements and are a vital part of helping them have an enjoyable experience with golf. If an adult has thrown a ball or simply attended a few PE classes at school, they likely have enough innate skills to swing a golf club. So, why are these innate movement skills often not present in the adult golf swing? Going back in time is particularly difficult and a more practical solution for the average adult is needed.

This burning question led me to study personal training; I couldn't articulate precisely why at the time, as I wasn't looking to change career paths to be a trainer. I felt that finding ways to improve golfers and re-capture their athleticism would require a practical and well-proven approach. Learning how the body works in a more general context led me to realise something that would prove pivotal. Golf coaches (myself included) have become so focused on analysing, critiquing and innovating golf swings that many well-established athletic training principles are being overlooked.

While playing in a golf tournament with another coach, in passing, I mentioned I was studying personal training; he responded dismissively, explaining that golfers don't want to be given an exercise program. I shrugged it off and proceeded anyway, with slightly less wind in my sails. My work with movement outside the context of a golf swing helped form much of the coaching philosophies I use today. I don't have a whistle and yell at people to do one more rep, nor a thriving golf personal training business. Instead, I developed ways to use golf to increase people's stability, strength and mobility in everyday life with the added bonus of enjoying a robust golf swing. Starting with athletic contentment has helped many clients feel there is a viable pathway to their goals.

Chapter 2
The Wall of Comfort

The wall of comfort is a metaphorical obstacle between you and your goals. The bricks in this wall are moulded from counterproductive habits, many stemming from failed attempts to improve. The hardest part of the process is that it's comfortable being in the shadow of the wall as it's a familiar place and you never quite know what's over the wall. Your plan of action could target the bottom few bricks while attempting to withstand them falling, alternatively, you could methodically take them from the top; it doesn't matter where you start, only that you do.

First, let's understand more about the origins of these habits that lead to the construction of the wall. The vast majority of our daily actions are done without thinking because habits run our lives. Repetition of anything breeds comfort and security even if it is against your best interests and you will need the right information to ensure that what you are chasing can be caught; herein lies the problem.

Sadly the primary information available is tips, tricks, secrets and shortcuts. Such big promises are seldom delivered upon. So why do these solutions rarely improve the average golfer? Golf improvement is messy and easily manipulated, leaving a big hole in the market, easily filled with expedient solutions. Consequently, the average golfer becomes conditioned to pursue a quick-fix cure rather than first addressing their wall. The quest for the easy way out might appear like a shortcut, but in the end, it proves to be an arduous and fruitless journey.

Making a change to be more productive can be scary, but I assure you it gets easier. One only needs sufficient motivation to make a change. Convincing golfers to make such a bold move will require a compelling alternative, so I got to work finding one. In my search for answers, I expanded my scope to other sports and other aspects of life, believing that the data pool need not be limited to golf. Taking a broader look at skill learning helped me re-discover how to improve at golf. Many of my clients are successful business people, so naturally, I asked them for advice. A common theme was to go ahead and start something, be it imperfect, make mistakes, and learn. Not only is this more fun, but much more effective than writing ten business plans and hoping to discover a golden goose while developing only the skill of writing business plans. Sound advice, I thought, and awfully applicable to the pursuit of better golf.

When you are ready to start improving, you must first prepare to learn. This involves looking inward, honestly, and assessing whether your expectations are aligned with reality. Take a step back, look around and try to understand what is reasonable, given the time, effort and experience you have to invest in improving your golf in targeted areas. If you have reached a reasonable competency in other sports, you are correct in thinking that will help your golf, however, it's best to leave that aside and allow that experience to help out if you re patient. You can say that you have very low expectations, yet your actions suggest very high expectations; this is a surefire way to become very frustrated.

A person aspiring to achieve something difficult should expect their time to be divided into three possible states; good performance, average performance and bad performance. Their actual ability isn't defined by any one of these states. Developing a feeling of entitlement to your "good performance state" beyond one-third of the time will result in an undeserved sense of disappointment. Not even the most resilient minds can take that much negativity.

On the other end of this scale is the euphoria felt when you just can't seem to miss as you stare down the flag. Unfortunately, this feeling inevitably slips away when the mojo wears off, adding to the collection of times the mojo evaded your grasp. To better manage yourself you can think of these moments as waves. A surfer recognises that they cannot control the waves. That perfect wave is an unparalleled experience where everything feels easy, and everything seems to work. When they jump off that wave, they are faced with a choice. Wait for the next perfect wave or carry on riding less perfect waves in preparation for the next time a perfect wave rolls in. The next time that perfect wave arrives in golf, first, enjoy the moment, then start preparing for the next one. This is true in most sports; a home run hitter in baseball cannot expect the same pitch and result from the next time they come to bat. They can simply enjoy the feeling while rounding the bases and return to the business of hitting the next time they come to the plate.

Golf has a unique ability to amplify human emotions. One of the more dramatic of these is frustration; it is an unavoidable part of golf and even serves as a motivator to improve. However, it can also corrupt your decision-making and needlessly make a bad situation much worse.

Knowing what to expect from your different clubs will save you from needless frustration.

The upcoming graph highlights how the club choice dictates how close the shot will get to the target. Most understand that a 4 iron is more difficult than a pitching wedge; however, it pays to recognise to what degree.

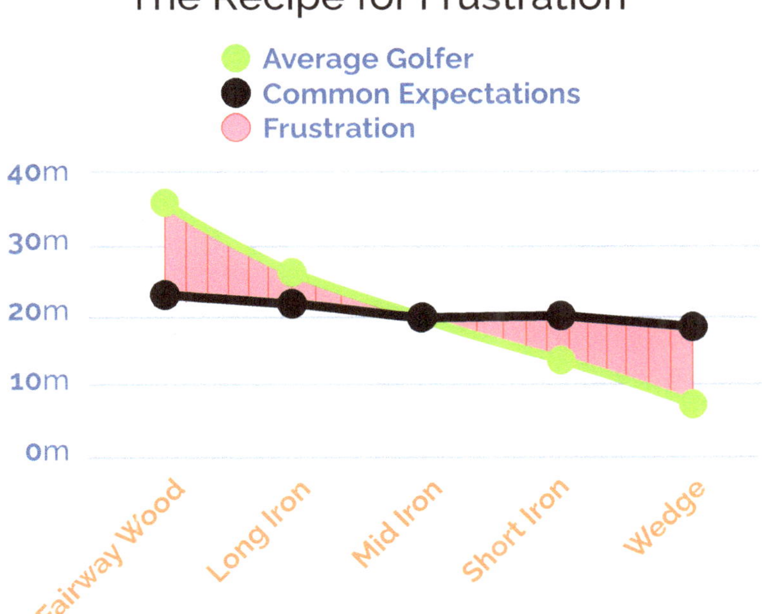

Data on accuracy of approach shots from Trackman available at www.trackman.com

The black line depicts an example of a common perception that the club choice will have a more negligible effect. It is the disparity between reality and expectations that result in frustration; luckily, your expectations are subjective and can be mitigated by continuously acknowledging the difference in difficulty. This works both ways as you can benefit from having higher expectations of shorter clubs.

With expectations closer to reality, opportunities to build confidence will undoubtedly present themselves. I like to think of these as opportunities for bravery. Bravely overcoming a challenge is the ultimate confidence builder. There is, however, an important distinction between brave and stupid: brave needs a reasonable chance of success and some trained competence. If you attempt something far beyond your competency, you might get lucky, however, this could bring with it a significant spike in emotions that will have you seeking increasingly risky situations to get the same experience, creating increasingly volatile shots. Making brave changes will be an uncomfortable experience, given you are breaking away from the sense of comfort built from familiar actions. You will, therefore, need some resilience and competence to help you push through. To build competence deserving of resilience, you will need to find a reliable source of information. Start by simply not taking every piece of information as fact before asking questions. Firstly, consider what is the reason for this proposed remedy? For example, if you are told to change your grip and the reason presented is simply because it's "correct", this stems from a version of logic that suggests having the correct grip inherently creates overall improvement. However, this logic hasn't considered your unique situation and may prove ineffective.

Provided the information is sound, there is still a cost-benefit analysis needed. Imagine you are at the range and observe that your trail hand is very much under the grip (you can`t see any knuckles), and the ball goes very far to the left when you hit it. When you manage to direct it at the target, it has a disappointing connection with the ball. When you place the trail hand in a more standard grip, the ball goes toward the target more often. This is when you need to take a moment to consider how much time and effort is needed to invest in making this promising change usable under pressure. Simply changing your grip without a plan to build competency will not work as this is not brave, just stupid.

Chapter 3
Is It My Tools?

It is essential to understand the role of your equipment in your golf experience. This doesn't mean you have to go and buy the latest and greatest clubs from companies that claim to have developed revolutionary new technology each and every year.

A builder will likely have a hammer and a nail gun and use both depending on their needs. Now, if you handed this builder a rock and said a poor tradesman blames his tools, he could hammer in the nails, but it would take longer, wouldn't be much fun, and the outcome would be less than that of using the proper tools. Where it gets a little unclear for the average person is adding the necessary context and details. If you consider that this same builder is on a small island and does not have a hammer, his only choice is a rock, and suddenly your view on using the rock changes drastically. If you are lucky enough to have the means to obtain tools beyond the metaphorical rock, you are best to ask yourself what tool is fit for your purpose.

To illustrate, take a handyman that has multiple projects planned over the next few years. He has some extra free time and is excited to spend it doing some DIY around the house. Fortunately, he has the financial means to purchase good-quality tools, but instead, he elects to use an old hand saw and hammer borrowed from a neighbour. The project is very demanding, and the handyman becomes increasingly frustrated to the point

Sam Hale

he eventually quits in a fit of rage. The handyman returns the tools to his neighbour, who is happy to have them back as he has been meaning to complete an odd job at his own house. The neighbour completes his job and is relieved he didn't buy any extra, fancier tools, which would likely be condemned to a future on a shelf collecting dust.

The average golfer`s golf club purchasing decision shouldn't be based on skill level; in fact, it's the lower-skilled golfer that benefits the most from purchasing better clubs. Like any other purchase, it comes down to how much you can afford, how often you intend to use them and the level of performance you intend to achieve.

The other essential tool for your golfing performance is the golf swing itself. Sadly many golfers sell themselves short of their potential, believing that their swing is working for them and it's simply a lack of mental fortitude or practice that stands between them and their goals. This could be the case, or they could merely be upset that their swing doesn't perform to a level conducive to their goals.

For example, Bob doesn't hit the ball very well, but the lack of distance lends itself to hitting more fairways and avoiding trouble; his short game takes up the rest of the slack, allowing him to score fairly well.

Rob has a great golf swing and slightly worse short game and mental skill level. The two players have played together several times and shot the same score. Bob and Rob get along well and decide to play weekly, then add up their points at the end of the year and award a prize to the winner. Rob will probably win despite his inferior short game and mental skills. Bob's mental fortitude and short game can only make up for a bad golf swing for so long before it fails to bridge the gap. Mental skills are a vital part of being a successful golfer. Yet, no amount of meditation, affirmations, hypnotism, breathing exercises and self-awareness can truly make up for a bad golf swing.

The way you interact with information is a key to understanding where to focus your efforts; the term keep it simple comes to mind as a very common nomenclature, especially in golfing circles. However, it is often misapplied by oversimplification and lack of consideration. When a proposed solution is overly simplified, it can lead to a complex and confusing experience. Another common saying that comes to mind is, "if it sounds too good to be true, it usually is". The best solutions have undergone great consideration and testing before being presented in a palatable way to your average golfer. Even if information comes from an experienced coach and communicator, it's not possible for a beginner or intermediate golfer to accurately process instructions and act on them in only a few short seconds. It is tempting then to simplify it into something immediately actionable, but doing so risks a lack of results and future confusion. Instead, take a few seconds to think, then pick something that resonates with you and just go with it. Let yourself fail; it's a great way to get better.

Chapter 4
The Fundamentals Of Golf

Imagine you are a total beginner golfer, so naturally, you seek advice from friends, family and the internet, where there proves to be no shortage of advice. As a logical person, something named fundamentals sticks out to you as a great place to start. After all, it's in the name. You are taught the correct grip, set up, ball position and alignment. You are also given some tips that, when done correctly, will all but ensure a successful shot. Keeping your head down seems a particularly promising prospect, and keeping your lead arm straight is a close second. As the primary advice you have received at this point, it sits at the forefront of your mind. When the associated results don't come, it could be a matter of more practice, but it also might have been doomed from the start.

Why is this not working for you? Well, these fundamentals and bonus tips weren't made for you. Traditional fundamentals originate from great golfers with status, expressing the importance of factors they believe are fundamental to their consistent performance. Of course, who wouldn't want to emulate the greatest players of all time? It makes sense to the average golfer to attempt to emulate what is fundamental to a great golfer's game and, therefore, a logical place to start.

One definition of fundamental is "a central or primary rule or principle on which something is based". To discover what this might be in golf is best done by searching for commonalities between great golfers. Feelings and intentions are very subjective, so an interview will be of little benefit in this area. It is more important to objectively observe movement skills. Grip, posture, ball positions, range of motion and tempo vary substantially among good players therefore such things clearly aren't inherently fundamental.

I divide fundamentals into two categories: traditional and movement. Traditional fundamentals refer to aspects such as grip, posture, ball position and alignment. Movement fundamentals include thoracic rotation, hip rotation, balance, sequencing and proprioception. Traditional golf fundamentals and movement fundamentals together make for a robust combination. When people are underperforming, it is likely because their movement fundamentals require attention. Sadly when traditional fundamentals are haphazardly applied, the golfer tends to fixate on these instructions, and their bodies will create compensating actions by sacrificing their movement fundamentals to hit the desired shot.

People who get off to a poor start are often given traditional fundamentals or tips as a remedy. When it does not serve as one, it leads to thinking of themselves as lacking in natural talent, as their efforts to improve have not come with the proposed performance gains while sensing a void in their athletic development. Scores can still be improved with intensive practice routines and number crunching for those particularly motivated, yet their potential will still feel unrealised.

Consistently Embracing Inconsistency

The best golfers in the world have a very consistent-looking swing. Although to them, it often feels quite the opposite because they are hyper-aware of the subtle differences in every shot. Tiger Woods once said he only feels like he has one or two good swings in each round of golf. When I was much newer to golf, I would watch a professional in awe, jealous of the seemingly effortless and consistent golf swing. Later, when I became a high-level golfer, I realised that looks can be deceiving. The spectrum of emotions, however, remained the same; I was mad at bad shots and happy at the good ones. The only difference was that the good and bad shots were objectively much better. Higher performance may not feel like you imagine it would; in fact, increasing your awareness of your faults is an integral part of the learning curve, but it is inherently an uncomfortable experience. Many remain in their comfort zone, writing it off as a lack of time or interest. This could be true, or they could be coping with failure by telling themselves they never wanted to succeed in the first place, a necessary coping mechanism in many areas but will need to be explored in order to move forward in golf.

Those who have allocated large chunks of time to practising (myself included) can likely attest that time practising does not necessarily make you better. There are many reasons for this, but perspective is a place to start. For example, one trap is perceiving golf as a fixed sport, implying that a good strategy is to repeat the same swing every time. Ironically attempting to do so will only create compensations that gone unnoticed long enough will be stored in muscle memory. In a round of golf, every shot is vastly different. The ball will be placed slightly differently in relation to you every time, as rarely is a fairway perfectly level nor the grass consistent. Beyond this, the variables include but are not limited to, wind, temperature, altitude, moisture , trees, hazards, bunkers, grass length, green softness, grass damage, green size, green shape, grain direction, and flag location.

Let's compare this to tennis, a sport that seems more fluid as there is a lot of running and limited time to think before you must react to the ball flying at your head. For the best chance of a successful return, players must first position themselves in a good place to swing relative to the ball and then their practised action will kick in to hit that ball back while their eyes are scouting where to put it relative to the opponent. The quality of practice dictates the effectiveness of the action in the moment.

PGA tour highlight reels are filled with pros getting in precarious situations and escaping by contorting their bodies. This isn't as difficult as it looks; it merely requires practice and placing your body in a position to hit. If a golf ball was thrown at you and you swung at it, you would have a reasonable chance of hitting it as hard as it may seem. This is because our subconscious is much better at golf than our conscious mind. Afterall, we can drive to work daily in a tin can on wheels at speeds that would make our caveman ancestors faint. We do such a difficult and dangerous task easily because of practice and experience, not with driving hacks or the latest innovative method. The principles are the same on the golf course; we just enjoy the advantage of the ball not moving and usually no threat of death, even if some people's emotional displays suggest otherwise.

We can capitalise on this extra time by creating rituals and a functional backswing designed to optimally position to hit the ball with a practised action. Why does golf feel so different to this? Golf provides a unique opportunity to ignore its fluid nature. While your conscious brain is trying to repeat the same swing every time, your body, unbeknownst to you, is employing compensating actions to hit the desired shot.

To start fresh, embrace the fluidity of golf. It can be liberating to know something many do not. Having the edge over your peers may help you enjoy the journey a little more. It's important to note that you do not require a deep understanding of a golf swing concept to perform it. A baby does not need to know the biomechanics of walking to achieve it. With this in mind, it's time you wipe the slate clean.

Creating a reaction void will allow your most universally utilised movements to take their rightful place in your golf swing. This process begins by choosing your pre-shot favourite movement fundamental from later in this book. Make your best effort to let go and ignore what happens to the golf ball; electing instead to focus your attention on your body. Doing so will form a bubble insulating yourself from the outcome. This may leave you in a rather uncomfortable mental battle; your old habits will jump in to drag you back to your comfort zone under the guise of "fixing" things. Take a second to re-engage with the task (it only takes 5 minutes of total commitment to alter your perspective). As you progress, letting yourself momentarily out of your bubble to enjoy the outcome is a helpful respite and moving in and out of the process bubble will help prepare you for the golf course.

A plan to develop competence will require resilience to survive dips in performance. Recognition that a dip is not a regression motivates you to stick to the task, not forever but only after giving it a chance could you deem it ineffective; if that's the case, you have still taken an opportunity to train your resilience, and your time will be well spent.

Using resilience to progress

Sam Hale

Chapter 6

Remembering Muscle Memory

Improving your game is a long-term investment; as such, you should do your due diligence to ensure a good potential for returns. In the quest for improvement, the 10,000-hour rule is heavily referenced, stipulating that it takes 10,000 hours to master something. I know plenty of people who have invested this amount of time, yet very few are masters. This suggests something is going wrong.

I remember learning about muscle memory in my high school sports science class. It's a well-established piece of science, yet golf has a unique ability to help us forget such rational memories. A strategy that seems to have taken its place is to try and hold on to the feeling of a good shot in the hopes of replicating it enough times that it will be stored as muscle memory. Unfortunately, this doesn't work because memories of feelings are unreliable and will obscure over a short time. After all, the point of training is to evolve something that feels uncomfortable to be comfortable, making for a different feeling. Re-discovering basic, proven principles has been one of the simplest yet effective things I've done in my coaching career.

When faced with a task, our brain looks to find the quickest and most efficient route to achieving it. This can be our downfall when we presume the goal is to learn the position or technique as quickly as possible to reap the associated benefits sooner, a little like my cat.

How does a human ensure the desired skills become muscle memory?

Muscle memory is formed from repetitions over time. There are three stages to building muscle memory: cognitive, associative and autonomous. First, you need to build awareness and control of movement. In other words, building a connection between your brain and a targeted area, so that you may stimulate and control that area more easily and precisely. You use this as your primary feedback in performing an appropriate amount of repetitions to progress from the cognitive to the associative stage of learning. The cognitive stage requires tremendous attention and will be the biggest test.

An indicator of being in the associative stage is when you require much less attention to perform the task. However, you will encounter a mental battle as you will likely try to circumvent the muscle memory process by simply dispelling the attention and believing you have made it to the associative stage after a few swings. The best practice is to keep doing cognitive level training over a few days to sure up the link between your mind and the targeted area. A connection will form either way, but this is an opportunity to ensure you only have to do it once. You can`t force muscle memory to kick in. It has a mind of its own, so to speak. For example, when you`re learning to ride a bike, each movement is thought out, peddling, maintaining your balance and using the brakes to stop. Over time, as you practise riding, your muscle memory will take over and free your mind from focusing on each action.

The movement may not be exactly what you intended, but if it's patiently trained, you will gain control and then fine-tune it later. The improvement process itself becomes more accessible after the first few attempts. Reaching the autonomous stage of learning can't be done just in the practice arena. It takes too long, and for it to hold up long-term, this new skill must be used at at every level of intensity. Progressive exposure to more stressful environments helps to transition from Assioative to Autonomas. The bridging process will be discussed in greater detail in the coming chapters.

Skill Funnel

Chapter 7

Swinging Your Swing

Golf has a long and rich history of playing host to various successful swing techniques. Swing attributes reflect the personality and the individual journey of a golfer. Someone who walks faster will often have a fast swing tempo and vice versa. Other characteristics of the swing will need to match up with your tempo, which contributes to the unique identity of a golf swing; what really matters is if it fits the user's needs. Tiger Woods is on to the fifth golf swing of his career, and I'm often asked why such a dominant golfer would change his swing? It's frustrating for a high-level golfer to visualise a cheque that their technique can`t cash. Another factor is that the maintenance of a golf swing or performance requires actions to improve, offsetting the natural regression that comes from the same old practice.

Since modern golf began, opinions on how best to swing the golf club have not been in short supply. I have spent years being an enthusiastic student of the golf swing. In my lifetime alone, I can recall being influenced by the One Plane swing, Natural Golf, Stack and Tilt, "A" swing, Moe Norman, Ben Hogan Fundamentals and many more. A more recent trend of note is promoting lead wrist flexion early in the swing, seemingly assuming that reducing face rotation overall will make for a more consistent face angle at impact (the Dustin Johnson type swing). A fine-sounding

Sam Hale

theory, yet I have witnessed nothing but compensations when the body senses a closed club face early in the swing. To be safe, I try to look at the rules, not the exceptions. Discussing and dissecting these different styles would be a whole other book, probably an interesting read for some but does little for the average golfer. So I'll leave that discussion there as I have chosen to pursue exactly what might help the average golfer truly learn from legends of the game.

Historically variations of a traditional two–plane swing have served the majority of successful golfers well for hundreds of years. I also think it suits the needs of the widest variety of golfers. A simple explanation of a two-plane swing is that the club rises above the original shaft plane on the back swing and then travels back down to the ball, reaching a similar orientation to which it started. A more singular plane style is easier for the observer's eye to track, however it can be more complex than it looks to execute. Such visual simplicity has proven easy to market over the years, backed up by the fact that the two-plane swing relies more on timing. I think a swing based on timing is a good thing; we have a better comprehension of timing than an imaginary line and leverage transferable skills that weren't learned via plane lines.

A more traditional two-plane swing best suits the development of movement fundamentals. It can be easily adjusted later to suit you or your coach's preferences. As the cognitive learning process is best done at a very low speed, it's best suited to lift your arms high enough to allow gravity to return the club back down. This creates an opportunity to build up your subconscious sense of where the club is relative to your body and, by proxy, in space. There shouldn`t be great tension in your arms at impact, as you wouldn`t expect it while releasing the ball from your hand during a throw; to do so would reduce speed and cause injury. The arms appear extended at impact because the club is heading very fast away from your centre toward the ball, not from excessive arm extension. It's a bit outside of my scope, but I suspect this significantly contributes to golfers' elbow and rotator cuff injuries, as you are effectively punching the ground via the club.

Chapter 8

Are You Out Of Your Mind?

Contrary to popular belief, it's not as desirable as you might think to hit the ball straight. Besides being nearly impossible, a fixation on hitting it straight is responsible for some of the worst swing compensations I have witnessed. The most prominent marker of an accomplished golfer is a somewhat consistent connection with the golf ball and a predictable outcome. To hit the ball too straight creates a two-way miss, which is undesirable because a golfer needs to consider and predict what will happen when they fail to produce a perfect shot. The average golfer's time might be better spent building movement fundamentals first than using traditional fundamentals to improve the distribution and predictability of the results. Predictability is essential to navigating the golf course efficiently.

Those debilitating nerves that you feel on the first tee or hitting in front of people are not something you can wave off at that moment. It comes down to preparation. Everyone has been in a situation where they react to a problem calmly and pragmatically and, conversely, been in one where they reacted poorly. The difference between these situations is often experience. This principle, unfortunately, works both ways. If you respond poorly to a particular situation, it becomes a habit to react that same way next time. This forms what's known as a mental block which will only be further reinforced if not addressed.

The good news is that habits can be changed. First, you find areas of improvement and get to work building competence. Then we must look for opportunities to exhibit bravery and confront the block. This is where you have to pick your battles. Don't reach for too much too early; nobody's confidence can withstand that. For example, you get a golf lesson the day before a tournament or big game. You are so excited by the proposed technical improvement that you decide to be "brave" and fully commit by sticking with "it" during your next round. This falls short because your body and mind don't fully understand what "it" is yet. Even the best technical solution in a stressful environment won't perform as it did when a comfortable environment is ideal for applying your full attention inward. On the golf course however, your attention is needed outwardly to deal with the many variables of every golf shot. Simply put, this technical improvement is not ready to play in the relative big leagues.

Instead, you should look to play what's in front of you when you play golf, not play golf swing. There will always be an element of something not quite ready and having to manage bad shots. The sooner you make peace with that, the more prepared you are to move forward slowly but surely. Once you have completed some quality practice, you can start by pretending you are in a stressful situation and take that opportunity to be brave. In trying the new skills in said situation, it's most important to accept the consequences. Likely, it won't go very well at first. This is where you will need your resilience until it gets easier. Once you have conquered this hurdle, you will need to step it up a notch; a great intermediary is to go and play golf by yourself with the express intention of confronting your mental blocks.

At the core of a robust mental game is the pre-shot routine: a ritual you have done many times before, akin to what athletes do to get them ready to perform. The purpose is simply to process and take action. The time this takes varies depending on what needs to be considered for each unique situation. Once the decision is made, you need only remind yourself of a couple of movements you prepared earlier. Since the feel is generated each time by specifically chosen movements, it forms a reliable method of positively interacting with your muscle memory to produce a predictable result. Line yourself up, aim and shoot. This should only take 10-20 seconds and the more efficient you become at this process, the more information you can process, resulting in better decisions. A well-implemented process that has been rehearsed will take up much less time than a few arbitrary practice swings and excessive time staring and wriggling around searching for the proper thought or feeling that worked previously.

Individuals have different speeds of processing information, as each situation has unique challenges. There is no set length of a pre-shot routine. To apply a set time limit will likely lead to missing something. Nobody wants to be that annoying golfer that takes forever to hit, nor fall victim to rushing and making a mistake. Like anything, the pre-shot process should be practised, creating a mental safe haven and allowing for clarity under pressure.

Chapter 9

OK, Im Ready! But Where Do I Start?

I am clearly of the opinion that many golfers needlessly fall short of their potential. Understanding and implementing movement fundamentals is a great place to start getting out of your own way. Like anything, it's not a catch-all solution. It does, however, have a remarkable ability to flush out compensations and clarify what might be the primary contributor to your lack of consistency or particularly undesirable outcomes.

For example, if someone has a "strong grip", it's likely that to hit the ball at the target, they are dropping their trail shoulder or even falling backward at impact to compensate, rendering their connection with the ball inconsistent. After working on their movement fundamentals, the ball will likely consistently go to the left. The advantage now is that you could make the grip more standard and get the ball heading toward the target with a more consistent connection. The key is creating an incentive to change the grip by ensuring it comes with a somewhat positive outcome. Getting to this point requires the user to get comfortable being uncomfortable. The main asset at this point will be the resilience to ignore the bad outcome long enough to get results. In my experience, it takes less than 10 minutes for those with a high tolerance for failure. For those lesser in that area, you can start building competence in your movement fundamentals to reduce the level of bravery required to let go.

A journey of 10,000 steps starts with just one step in the right direction. Take your time deciding what your first action will be. Talk to a coach, do some testing and once you have chosen a target set a time frame to apply total commitment. This doesn't guarantee immediate improvement, as that is subject to the suitability of the information. There will never be a guarantee of spectacular golf shots in any one practice session, but you can guarantee overall progress by committing to the task. It's much easier said than done, and you will want to retreat back to comfort after a few shots. Try to see this coming, take a second and remind yourself of the purpose of the session.

Years of inconsistency and confusion can lead many to see their golf swing as a fragile flower knocked over by a stiff breeze, as if the ball position being a little off or not hitting a backswing position will be the difference between success and failure. It doesn't have to be that way, and there is a way forward. I'm fairly confident that you don't wake up some mornings and forget how to drive. At the same time, if your expectations of yourself are so high that you attempt to drive like an F1 driver on the way to work, you will likely get into trouble. Quality practice will produce a robust sporting technique that you own. How effective it becomes depends on how well you apply yourself to developing your movement and traditional fundamentals.

Chapter 10

Constants Of Coordination

A level of coordination is needed to effectively use tools like training aids, video analysis and swing plane guides. Ironically those most likely to seek help from these are also the least likely to benefit. The interventions mentioned above can be highly beneficial when you have control and awareness of the areas the chosen intervention intends to adapt. When sufficient control or awareness isn't present, you will compensate with what you can control. A strong connection between your brain and the area that controls the desired movement is an essential prerequisite to changing a movement habit. For this you will need a constant and reliable reference point from which to base your actions and progression; What something feels like moment to moment is anything but constant, so we are best served to start with the biggest constant of them all, gravity. Your relationship with gravity is measured by your sense of balance and via actions that are not fighting against it. Maintaining balancing during movement occupies your smaller muscles while freeing up your bigger muscles to generate speed as they are wasted trying to keep you balanced. Secondly, by allowing gravity to influence the club at different points of the swing, you can increase your innate sense of where the club is in relation to yourself and space.

Movements need to be performed slowly with particular attention to what controls the movement; everything else needs only come along for the ride. Each repetition should be done with the same amount of care and time. Developing control of the movement will allow you to perform it faster and more smoothly. Attempting to make it fast or smooth before control is established will severely compromise the results. There are two key areas the following training is designed to improve, which are body coordination and hand-eye coordination. Body coordination refers to your body movements relative to itself and gravity (movements relative to gravity are represented by balance). Additionally, hand-eye coordination refers to using said coordination to interact with something outside of your body, i.e. hitting a golf ball.

The Sam Hale Golf C.F.A system ensures the correct muscles are being activated at the right time to ensure accuracy of movement.

The C.F.A system is based on the following key definitions:

Controller: Primary muscle(s) that your attention is connecting with to power the movement.
Follower: Allows the controller to lead while staying relaxed and passive.
Anchor: A reference to avoid compensation.

Cues are designed to activate the group of muscles best suited to perform the movement. Think of your brain and your attention as the conductor and your body as the orchestra. The conductor directs in a way that produces the desired outcome, but it takes practice, after which the orchestra and conductor will more easily learn other pieces of music. In time they become able to pay some attention to their surroundings. That's where you need to get to before hitting the golf course.

Structured vs Unstructured

Structured training isn't everyone's cup of tea, but if you are particularly organised, you could try the following exercises in sets and reps. Or alternatively you may proceed at your own pace and simply ensure you have regular mental and physical breaks. Having a structure to your training helps distribute your effort through reps, sets and the duration of a rep, but you can take the same principles and apply them more fluidly. The most important principle is the rep duration, as you will likely try and speed up. Maintaining a consistent rep length ensures the appropriate level of attention is allocated to each rep. If the reps speed up, it`s probably not a sign of progression; it's more likely a lack of attention, given you are in the cognitive stage of learning.

Stage 1
Upper Body

Standing straight up and down in balance, fix the lower body (Pelvis) and rotate the upper body (Upper Spine/Thoracic). Keep the head facing forward with the neck and shoulders relaxed and hands on the golf club.

Considerations

Your shoulders can move and give the appearance of the upper body rotating, so it's important to use the sternum as a reference. Don't be surprised if there is very little range of motion. This isn`t a big deal, quality over quantity.

Controller: Sternum

Anchor: Hips

Follower: Neck Muscles

Stage 2
Arm lift

Place your shoulder blades against a wall, lift your arms with your shoulders while keeping your biceps, forearms and wrists relaxed.

Considerations

Keep your lower back close to the wall. Take this slow and engage your shoulders. Drop your arms by releasing your shoulders so your hands lightly tap the wall at the bottom.

Controller: Shoulders

Anchor: Shoulder Blades/ Thoracic

Follower: Arms

Sam Hale

Stage 3
Dynamic Set-Up

Stand up straight and in balance, hinge at the hips while keeping your legs straight and allowing the weight to move to your toes. Then bend your knees slightly, resulting in the weight being more toward the middle of your feet. Relax your shoulders and arms and let them hang. Where the club is located in relation to you is where it should be, tiptoe toward the ball while maintaining your structure.

Considerations

Every detail of this protocol is equally important. It is best to start slightly too far from the ball to ensure you don't have to tiptoe backward to establish the right distance.

Controller: Hips

Anchor: Feet

Follower: Arms

Stage 4
Upper Body

Set up in golf posture and then rotate the upper body while keeping the lower body fixed and head facing forward with neck muscles and shoulders relaxed.

Considerations

Keep arms relaxed and allow them to travel with the sternum. The lead arm can press against chest slightly for "correct" sequencing.

Controller: Sternum

Anchor: Lower Body/ Head

Follower: Arms/Neck

Stage 5
+Lower Body

Rotate the upper body (Thoracic Rotation), then drop the lead shoulder slightly (Left side bend). Allow the hips to follow the control of the upper body.

Controller: Sternum

Anchor: Feet

Follower: Hips

Stage 6

+Arm Lift

Lift the arms in the same manner as on the wall (Stage 2).

Considerations

Focus on the specific movement from the shoulders rather than the fact that they are lifting because you are now in golf posture which means this movement lifts the club horizontally rather than straight up. Resist worrying about positions or steepness/shallowness as it's dictated by how all of these movements interact, not by your arms.

Controller: Shoulders

Anchor: Sternum

Follower: Rest of Arm

Stage 7
+Arm Drop

From the top of the backswing (Stage 6), release your shoulders and allow your arms to float down.

Considerations

Avoid using your lats to pull your arms down. If you have hit a golf ball before, your upper body will instinctually rotate back to the target, so do not add this as a conative thought.

Controller: Gravity
Anchor: Sternum
Follower: Arms

Stage 8
Club Lift and Drop

Do stage 6 with a club in hand. During the backswing with no intervention, the club will want to tip behind you. Let it do so slightly. Then release your shoulders as in stage 7.

Considerations

Avoid using your lats to pull your arms down. It will feel strange as the club will seem to be headed in the wrong direction. Your upper body rotation is already muscle memory in some form. As you look at a golf ball, it will react to the club falling if you let it. Don't try and add this on as a swing thought. Your attention need only be on the shoulders releasing.

Controller: Sternum
Anchor: Shoulders
Follower: Arms

 Sam Hale

Stage 9
Hand-Eye Coordination

From a pause at the top, check your balance, then direct your attention to releasing your shoulders. While also looking at the golf ball but with no express intention to actually hit it.

Considerations

You may miss the ball the first few times. Stick to the task; you will adapt appropriately rather than compensate. If you are still unsuccessful after giving it a fair chance, then return to the earlier steps to build competence.

Controller: Gravity

Anchor: Sternum

Follower: Arms

But how do I hit the ball?

Thoracic rotation will engage itself, pulling the club toward the ball, and hand-eye coordination takes care of the rest. For example, what would you do if you were at the top of your backswing and someone took the club from you and replaced it with a ball, instructing you to throw it toward the target? You would likely use your innate skills to enact a throwing motion toward the target and likely even lead with your hips (correct sequence). Be careful not to overthink it by trying to piece together each proceeding action mentally to be able to do it; quite the contrary.

Integrating Traditional Fundamentals

Traditional fundamentals are now a tool to refine your swing. If the results are suitable to your needs after working on your movement fundamentals, then you need only familiarise yourself with your current traditional fundamentals and keep them in check. Start with attention to how you grip the club and feel it in your fingers. Be aware of what your back feels like in your posture and where your shoulders sit. Tune in to where exactly you are aiming relative to the target, a little left and a little right. No need to fix it. We don't want your grip, setup, or other vital things to change without notice. It is worth noting that most of this should be done off the ball and ideally in practice first. You have likely heard the idea of taking your time on the range or course; that time isn't for problem-solving; it is for some ritualistic checks. Experience has taught the excellent player that trouble could be coming for your golf swing when your grip, posture or ball position changes inadvertently.

If your results are still unsuitable for your needs, you should contact a local PGA coach or contact me personally. You and your coach will look into how your swing works and what needs changing to complement what you have. There are likely a few options with different pros and cons to consider, so it's always good to speak to an expert.

Building A Bridge Between The Driving Range And The Golf Course

So you`re on the driving range working on your swing; everything's going well, your swing changes are feeling more comfortable, and it starts to feel increasingly plausible that these changes will help you on the golf course. You take a few critical observations of what you believe to be most responsible for this increased performance and store them away. The next day rolls around, and you make your way to the golf course with high hopes. Once you arrive at the first tee and start to set up the golf ball, you try to remember some of the keys you had tucked away in your memory for this very situation and as your mind reaches around in the dark, you realise you are taking too long and quickly hit the shot. The round ends as a failed attempt at extending your driving range prowess to the golf course.

The first thing you need to do is bring your perception of your driving range ability back down to earth. What exactly are you considering a successful shot? You may settle for a nicely struck shot on the driving range, paying little attention to the target. You may even convince yourself that you meant to hit it there the whole time. To conserve your ego, your brain tends to tactically forget bad shots and instead focus on more pleasant experiences. Driving range mats are often cited as the main reason the driving range varies so much from the golf course, which is true, but they don't have to. The mat is flat and pointed in a consistent direction, implying a lack of variety and unrealistic results. It also allows the club to keep travelling toward the ball where it otherwise would have dug into the turf. Given time and attention, you can choose to be more attentive to the quality of the connection to the ball, allowing you to simply recognise that it wasn`t a good shot and resist patting yourself on the back. As for the direction of the mat, aim for different things. We often expect the environment to do the training for us. It's true that different environments inherently promote various aspects of training, yet it is far from guaranteed. What does ensure progress is challenging yourself regardless of your environment and then creating an environment as a bonus. The mindset of finding something to do the work for you extends to training aids, swing theories and golf clubs, all of which could be of great benefit if they are first recognised as merely tools to guide you. If it claims to do the work for you, or you see it as such, it won`t do its job. You could convince yourself it is working, provided you are particularly fond of walking in circles. Blending new skills into your golf game can play out differently for many people. For example, a player will often perceive that they have two swings at play if they have reworked and fixed their swing; the old and the new. This suggests that an exit strategy is possible by falling back on your old swing. This gets confusing because as the new swing becomes more of a habit, the old swing no longer feels the same, and it becomes difficult to discern between the old and the new. This can lead to distress when an otherwise helpful coping mechanism kicks in to selectively remember the good shots, making it especially hard to accurately assess which swing is more effective. To counter this, prepare for a forward-facing mindset and don't look back. You are better off committing to something and learning from it than constantly assessing and testing.

Where perceiving an old and new swing can be useful is to see the New Swing as a side project, recognising that it is not yet ready for any real pressure. You own a company, and the CEO (Old Swing) has served you well, but it's time for them to retire, and you see this as an opportunity to bring in a young person (New Swing) that has the potential to take the company to the next level. It's not wise to immediately insert them into this role as they are still a little young and inexperienced, they will improve eventually, but their confidence and the company's performance would suffer from such a reckless move. Instead, you elect to train them up until their competence is high enough to take over. There will always be somewhat of a leap when starting a new role regardless of competence, yet training them up as a side project makes for a smaller leap and a lower chance of failure. Once the new CEO has taken over, there is no turning back; your preparation has made you confident enough to ride out the bumps. Simply picking someone off the street to be your new CEO is akin to implementing a random tip.

To best prepare, you must first address how you percieve the golf swing and the task. The core identity of your golf swing is your muscle memory; this is what you are left with when your back is against the wall. This core is both maintained and positively and/or negatively influenced by associative and cognitive level muscle memory. To maintain what you have while slowly improving your core swing comes down to the quality of your initial training process and how it is bridged into your golf game.

When you have done the initial training of a new move, a great way to start to blend it into your golf swing is to set up a bit of a game with yourself. First, conduct the targeted movement using your awareness and control at what feels like 30% power, but with a full-length swing (Very Slow), the ball should only be nudged forward around 20 or 30 yards. Provided you feel you did a good job, you immediately visualise a bigger shot and attempt 60% power. If you are successful again, quickly go for 100% and beyond until failure, at which point you return to 30%. The ratio intended is to spend most of your time in the 30% zone to ensure quality. This is self-managed and subjective by design; your feeling of how coordinated and smooth it is will be your main feedback. It's integral to blasting through each level, not stopping to see if you can repeat a few 100 percenters in a row. Trying to replicate a 100% swing will bring in old thought patterns and make you overthink it. If you are patient, you will hit some of the best shots ever, seemingly deliberately. Don`t let great shots bait you into breaking away from the task. Take a second to enjoy the shot, then return to the game, as this is your best chance of enjoying the experience again.

The 30% swing serves an essential purpose

from now on; it becomes a method of ensuring that you are maintaining the quality of the movement, and it will serve as a very efficient practice swing. A meaningful practice swing reminds you and your body of an associative skill that is a high priority as it leads to a somewhat predictable result when added to your core swing. It's time then to put it through its paces by setting up varying situations on the driving range with progressive difficulty. Your brief yet concise practice swing is the extent of your technical thought. Once you get over the ball, you are ready to hit and accept the consequences, whatever they may be. This is likely to feel like a massive regression in your performance. It's not; keep going to get through the dip as it's better to fail here than on the first tee.

After some time building resilience and competence, you'll be excited to seek out the next challenge. Set up a relatively low-pressure situation like playing nine holes alone or with a good friend, so you aren't embarrassed to hit some bad shots. Mentally prepare to push through a perceived dip in performance. It will become much more comfortable, and your confidence will grow. Once you have moved through this process, you will start to free up some awareness to consider aspects that will improve your score.

Chapter 12

Play Smarter, Not Harder

How does one find the time to improve their golf in a time-poor and distracting world? Nobody seems to practise nearly as much as they want, and it doesn't seem to help when they do so I don't blame people for not bothering.

The good news is that the ideal facility to start your movement skill was right under your nose the whole time; it's your living room. A comfortable external environment is essential in adequately committing to leaving your internal comfort zone. When you arrive at the driving range or golf course, the environment has more significant external pressures. You will be internally more comfortable as you have done the movement many times in the comfort of your own home. You need only conduct your practised action while looking at a golf ball. This will be easier as at least the movement itself feels more comfortable so you are just left with allowing time for your hand-eye coordination to calibrate, so be patient. You can keep a club in the office as it makes for a great mental holiday from work, direct your mind to a specific movement skill for a short time, and then get back to the grind.

If you have watched golf on TV, you will notice that every golfer has some slightly unique rituals they do during their athletic pursuits. These rituals serve many purposes: a mental anchor that helps shift your mind into a state of purpose while performing on a golf course. It offers the opportunity to remind you of techniques you may be working on.

A pre-shot routine is made up of: observation, decision, swing preparation, aim and fire. With practice, your pre-shot routine becomes a highly effective method of processing information and decision-making, which is key to performing under stress. So when creating or improving your pre-shot routine, you should look to account for each stage, no more, no less. Most of the observation stage can be done before you get to the ball. You can check out the green, where the pin is, and what the wind is doing. Give some thought to what line you might want to take. This allows more time to make a good decision. At this point, commitment is of the utmost importance. If you find it very hard to commit, the shot you have chosen is likely beyond your competence. Consider adjusting your decision-making to promote a greater level of commitment.

Your swing will benefit from a slight jump start, courtesy of your practice swing. This is where your 30% swing comes in handy. Rehearse your 30% swing close to the ball, then set it up to the ball and fire away. Express some emotion if need be but try not to break anything or offend anyone. Then proceed to the next shot, where you will feel better once your pre-shot routine kicks in. The emotion from your last shot will drift away as you begin to make observations for the next shot.

When it comes to making good decisions, you learn to make better decisions through experience and accountability. It's not about making the perfect tactical decision. It's simply a case of noting and then committing to a conclusion. A lot of the time, your first instinct is best anyway. You learn a lot about

Sam Hale

your decision-making from a shot executed exactly as intended but with a bad outcome. There isn't much to learn from a perfect decision and lousy shot because you'll never know how it could have turned out. Since this is the case, thinking this way helps to take the emotional sting out of the bad outcomes, not because you are a zen master, but simply because you are too busy learning rather than concerning yourself with tantrums and self-pity.

Some consideration during your decision-making process should be given to managing risk. Without some risk, we don't get a reward, and we don't get to bravely overcome things. Too much risk, however, either leaves you very disappointed or, if all goes exceedingly well, the brain gets hit with an excessive shot of dopamine which will have you chasing that next hit and enduring disappointment from anything short of a god-like result. An individual's tolerance for risk can vary greatly, so this becomes a rather introspective and unique process for every golfer.

Directional Risk Management

Aiming straight at the cup is by no means inherently a silly play; however, in the situation displayed, it likely is. The wise play is splitting the difference and taking on a little risk.

Sam Hale

Distance control starts by observing the outcome of shots when your swing is most coordinated and smooth. Hopefully, it's not too straight, as this can make playing more challenging. We are looking to create two categories of the outcome: (I) represents your intended outcome and (M) represents the most common missed shot.

There are three hypothetical situations in the diagram that are classified as safe, smart or silly due to the unique risks of the situation.

Risk Reward

"Safe" represents the safest option, as all three possible outcomes result in no significant danger, although likely a more challenging next shot. The "silly" option leaves both of your potential missed shots in a bad situation.

.

Distance Risk Management

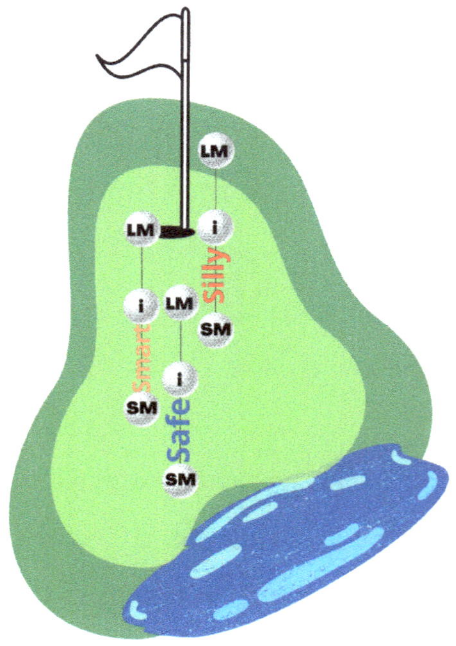

When making decisions about distance, the considerations are similar. As the diagram above shows, there is a long miss (LM), meaning the ball flew further than (I) intended, and a short miss (SM), which refers to the ball falling short of the target. The "safe" classification has all of these outcomes avoiding trouble. Silly would be going long on a back pin resulting in a highly challenging next shot and safe being well short of this. "Smart" is again effectively splitting the difference.

Chapter 13

Be A Golf Guide

Golf is a growing sport; many of your peers will likely come to you for advice. I like to think of this role as a golf guide; you can play your part by guiding them in the right direction. What you should avoid is being a swing instructor or swing coach. There is much more valuable work to do than critique the subtleties of their golf swing or list "faults" that you can observe. We know it's not a good thing to micromanage in business. A person needs to be allowed to make mistakes without expecting a critique every time; micromanagement isn`t a good idea in golf either. Your experience with the game of golf is your most valuable asset in helping someone else. This experience allows you to inform and shape their expectations. You mustn't encourage continual swing theories and you should always avoid presenting something as fact. If the mentee is particularly interested in the technical side, then discuss what you know about movement fundamentals as the true sign of competence in a subject is to recognise how much you still don't know, so don't be afraid to say you don't know the answer. It may seem easier in the moment to pass a guess off as fact. This is a very human reflex, and I myself have been guilty of this. I try to mitigate it by being self-aware and reminding myself that the purpose of coaching is to help them improve their golf, not to build my ego.

As a guide who knows this person better than most, you are best equipped to direct them to a coach or piece of information that suits their needs. You have ample opportunity to understand the landscape of golf improvement, and are therefore best equipped to guide them to success.

Chapter 14
Enjoy The Process

One of my biggest lessons in golf is learning to enjoy the process of getting better. You never stop learning and trying to improve. This game has brought me more emotion than any other area of my life. In recent years hitting golf balls has become one of the most calming things I do. I still get mad on the golf course, but over time I have learned not to dwell on this feeling, credited not to meditation or virtue, but because I have come to realise negative emotions will only hinder the performance at my next shot. Frustration is inevitable, and failure is expected. How you respond to these moments dictates how deeply they will affect your golf. If it becomes instinct to put more time and effort into quality practice, it becomes progressively easier to bounce back. The more memories you have of bouncing back, the more confident you will feel in a moment of pressure.

Trusting in a decision you have made is easier said than done; "Trust it" is a term thrown around, yet in practice, it seems to be a highly conditional trust. Meaning when the performance dips, many jump ship in search of the next thing to trust. This shallow deal can be replaced with a more productive alternative I call tactical commitment; this starts with allocating an amount of time to commit to something and being clear about what it will take to get there. Even if it proves to be an ineffective task, seeing it through will teach you something about where to go next and how to be better next time. It's a whole lot more fun and more productive than chasing lasers.

If you have made it this far, I thank you for your time and attention. It's important to note that you don`t need to understand every facet of what's been covered in this book to take a step forward; simply find a piece that resonates with you and apply it. You will likely form your own versions of the processes and perspectives I have shared with you better adapted to yourself. I thoroughly enjoyed the challenge of creating something I truly believe can help the average golfer get out of their own way.

About the Author

Sam Hale is the head coach at Golf HQ Takapuna in Auckland, New Zealand and the founder of Golf Rockers LTD.
He has been passionate about golf since he first picked up a club at age 13.
Now, as a PGA Professional Coach, he has the privilege of helping people get meaningful results.

www.samhalegolf.com
www.golfrockers.com

GOLF HQ

MIZUNO

PROFESSIONAL GOLFERS' ASSOCIATION
PGA
1913
NEW ZEALAND

GOLF ROCKERS

THE
GOLF
PHYSIO.

Notes:

 Sam Hale